To Mary's
Soul sisters

Blessings

IN LOVE WITH THE MYSTERY

Library and Archives Canada Cataloguing in Publication

Mortifee, Ann
    In love with the mystery / Ann Mortifee.

Accompanied by compact disc.
ISBN 978-0-9810065-0-5

    1. Self-realization. 2. Self-actualization (Psychology). 3. Meditations.
I. Title.

BF637.S4M677 2010   158.1   C2010-904455-X

Cover and book design: Diane Feught
Front cover photo: Courtney Milne

Eskova Enterprises Ltd. Vancouver, BC
2010 Eskova Enterprises Ltd.

PRINTED IN CANADA

IN LOVE WITH THE MYSTERY

────────

ANN MORTIFEE

────────

PHOTOGRAPHY BY COURTNEY MILNE

────────

ESKOVA ENTERPRISES LTD.

Foreword

Ann Mortifee is considered by many to be a truly renaissance woman. Her passionate fascination with spirituality, science and art has been a driving force throughout her life. Ever since she was a young girl, Ann has been beguiled by a persistent yearning to explore and engage in the mystery of life. This has been her muse, her companion and her most formidable teacher.

Ann has always followed her heart, even when her logical mind suggested she do otherwise. Her conviction to create art that expressed her deepest values meant that she often turned down career-advancing opportunities that promised conventional success. Instead, Ann used this same conviction as the impetus behind all of her expression: her extraordinary singing voice, her musical theatre productions, albums, ballets, film scores, storytelling, poetry, and the evocative keynote addresses and workshops presented at conferences and retreat centers throughout the world.

She has worked internationally with hospitals and hospice caregivers, serving the dying and those suffering through great loss. She has taught singing and creative expression as a way of opening emotionally to deeper expressions of self. She has served in the environmental movement, co-founding The Trust for Sustainable Forestry. All of this and more led to her work being recognized in her appointment to membership in the prestigious Order of Canada.

Years ago, Ann chose to begin awakening each morning at sunrise. During these hours of quiet, she developed a fertile stillness that has led to an ever-deepening awareness. Every passage in this book is testimony to Ann's commitment to this deep listening. Her words evoke a quickening through which we can awaken more fully to the gifts in ourselves. These passages are potent; one striking the heart like a gong, the next, as comforting as a lover's caress. I found them both heartbreakingly beautiful and liberating.

This is not a book about Ann, nor has it actually been written by Ann. Rather I see this as a book that has come through Ann as a simple offering from the heart.

Exquisitely sensitive photographs by Courtney Milne, acclaimed photographer and Ann's dear friend, complement the writings. Images and words flow together with magical symmetry thanks to the elegant design of Diane Feught.

On the companion compact disc, Ann's voice transports the listener to places where one can meditate on the wisdom within one's own heart. It was recorded with her husband, world-renowned flutist, Paul Horn. This inspired musical offering, a marriage of two visionary souls traveling together, is an added gift to be experienced alone or in union with the book.

I invite you to be awakened to your own voice through the words and music of *In Love with the Mystery*.

Nancy Fischer Mortifee

Also by Ann Mortifee

The Awakened Heart (with John Robbins)

Into the Heart of the Sangoma

When the Rains Come

Healing Journey

Serenade at the Doorway

Born to Live

Journey to Kairos

Reflections on Crooked Walking

Baptism

Ecstasy of Rita Joe Ballet

ACKNOWLEDGEMENTS

Every step in the creation of *In Love with the Mystery* has emerged on the wings of effortless surprise. I never intended these writings to become a book. It is to the following people that I owe my heartfelt love and thanks. Each has helped to imagine and birth the offering you now hold in your hands.

To Carol Sill for your kindly, precise and insightful vision in the editing of all that wanted to come. I have loved every brilliant moment of our journey together.

To Diane Feught, for creating such beautiful harmony. You have manifested from all the strands an exquisite weave, making our book so much more than the sum of its parts.

To my dear friends, Edward Henderson, Miles Black and Paul Baker, for each of your exquisite gifts of deep listening. Your sound and music lifted us to heights beyond where we could possibly have gone alone.

To my wonderful friends, Sherrill Miller and Courtney Milne, for so openly and generously sharing the magnificent creations from the eye of the master; yours is a gift from the gods.

To my wonderful brother, Peter Mortifee, for your love and for your grounded understanding of the ways of the world, which are so deeply supporting the unfolding of all my dreams.

To my dear sister-in law (or in heart), Nancy Mortifee, for your diligent, loving and graceful shepherding of each and every phase of this project. Without you it would not exist at all. You are a gift beyond measure in my life.

And first and last, to my beautiful husband, Paul Horn, for being the constant source of joy, inspiration and support that has birthed this new beginning. Your love has made every step of this lifetime a holy thing, knowing that it all has led to you. None of this would ever have happened without the healing balm of your love.

Ann Mortifee

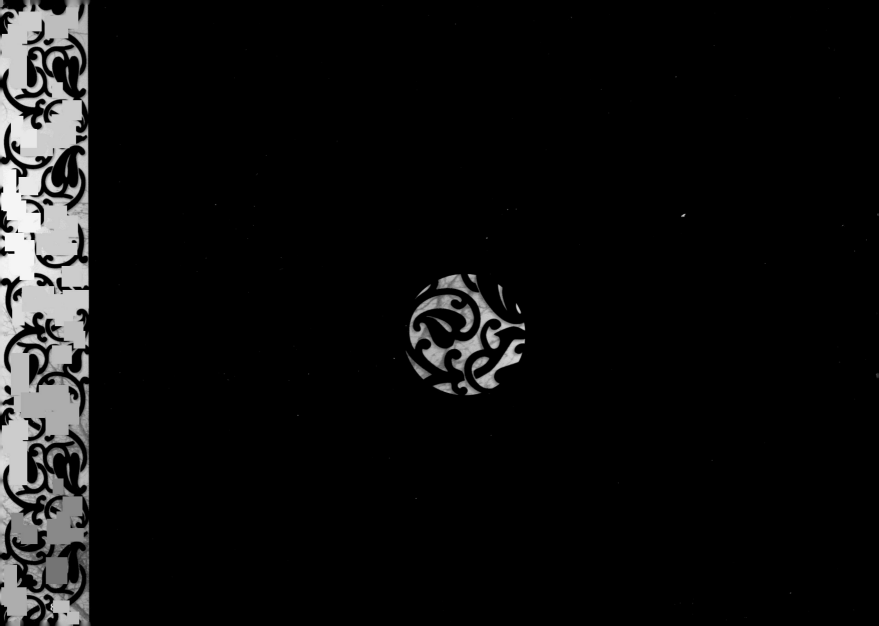

MYSTERIOUS JOURNEY

Mysterious Journey

When a path opens before us that leads we know not
where, don't be afraid to follow it. Our lives are meant
to be mysterious journeys, unfolding one step at a time.
Often we follow a path worn smooth by the many and
in doing so we lose our authenticity, our individuality,
our own unique expression. Do not be afraid to lose
your way. Out of chaos, clarity will eventually arise.
Out of not knowing, something new and unknown
will ultimately come. Do not order things too swiftly.
Wait and the miracle will appear.

THE JOURNEY OF UNFOLDING

What do we need in order to realize
there is a journey to be taken? What do
we fear that keeps us from taking it?
Go deeper! Find your will. Find your
love and your wisdom. Devote yourself
to the miracle that is you. Let your own
passion be the pressure that turns
carbon into crystal. There is no more
worthy or miraculous adventure than
the journey of unfolding.

THE SEED OF YOUR BECOMING

The beauty of a seed is its raw potential.
The wonder of a blue robin's egg, a green
sprout, the golden dawn of a new day –
all these remind us that a new beginning
is always at hand. Let each moment of
the year to come be filled with the wonder
that there is no past and there is no future.
There is only the glorious unfolding
of Now. Each moment, this moment
is the seed of your becoming.

Strange Nostalgia

A distant sound, the song of a bird, the whistle of a train, or a wolf's howl at midnight, often fills the heart with a strange nostalgia. A sense of far off places, vast expanses, calls us to come. For a moment our energetic awareness opens. We sense that we are more than the small self with which we so often identify. Suddenly, we yearn for that largess, that vastness of nature, which is the gift we receive in meditation. The small self dissolves and wc become one with the emptiness beyond space. We touch the essential Self for which we yearn.

Today is the Day

Today is the day to begin anew the great adventure. Today is the day to resolve to awaken in every moment. Today is the day to commit, to determine, to live, to love. This is the day in which to serve our highest dream. If we wait for circumstances to align in the way we desire, we may wait forever. Tomorrow is an illusion. Today is the day to breathe in the mysterious possibility that life now offers. Regardless of what surrounds us, this is the day to begin.

HERE AND NOW

Living in the present moment is
the only way to tame the mind.
For the mind throws us into turmoil,
thinking of the past and worrying about
the future. By noticing our breath,
the inner sensations of the body,
the light around us, the ground beneath
our feet, we begin to find ourselves in
the here and now. The question, "what if …"
ceases to plague our days, and acceptance
begins to flower.

A LIVING RELATIONSHIP

Every relationship flounders and grows
estranged if not given time and attention.
So it is in our relationship with the Unknown.
The more awareness we focus toward our
connection with the Great Mystery, the more
returns to us. We create a circuit of energy,
one that is vital and life-giving.
Our communications become clearer,
our awareness more aligned. Cultivate a living
relationship with the Unknown. And like all
relationships, it will grow and expand into
something splendid.

Soul's Communication

The soul communicates through feelings,
sensations and intuitions. Through these
we grasp the inner tuition by which
we learn. The soul does not speak
directly through the mind. Its wisdom
arrives in the emotional body and
then travels to the mind as a knowing.
The mind then analyzes what the sensing
body already knows. Quiet times of
listening, of being still within the body,
give access to the soul's communication.

Don't Wait

We must generate the life we desire.
We cannot base our actions on the actions
of others. We cannot wait for others to
be kind to us. We must offer kindness
to them first. Those who wait to find
someone deserving of their generosity
may wait forever. Life is not a matter
of deserving or not deserving. Life can
only become what we dream if we become
the expression of the dream we desire to live.
Don't wait. Become a transformative
force for good.

The Soul's Clarity

The purpose of the mind is to gather, receive and sort information. The ability to use that information to determine truth with insight and clarity is a higher function belonging to the Soul. Often we seek to determine with the logical mind alone. Without the soul's clarity, we are in danger of imposing, upon ourselves and others, a code of dogmatic morality. Principles and ethics are best developed and distilled by a reasoning mind and a feeling heart listening deeply to the expansive discernment of Soul.

The Doorway Now

Every moment is the opportunity to begin anew, so that life can be forever fresh and vital. Whatever it is that you have been chasing, let it wait. Don't force, allow. You will get there when the time is perfect and the way is clear. Don't rush, relax. Let the past drift away into what has been. Let the future take care of itself. This is the doorway now. This is the chance you have been waiting for.

The Law of Nature

We are never separate from what we
need for our unfolding. The energy
that creates every substance, animate and
inanimate, exists in the vibrating matrix
that surrounds and flows through us.
We can be assured that our prayer and
intention vibrates that creative energetic
web to attract to us and to manifest our
Highest Good. What we call faith is
a deep trust in this power of attraction,
a knowing that when we focus our
consciousness with energy toward what
we need, the Law of Nature always responds.

Source of Power

As one would face the morning sun,
confident in its illuminating light,
so we look to our Higher Nature confident
that it will bring insight and inspiration.
We are connected to a Source of Power
that never sets. It is always present and
shining, even when it appears to have
gone beyond our conscious awareness.
We have only to be confident in this
Source of Power, for our True Self to
enlighten us with the wisdom we need
to light our way.

The Lens of the Mind

The mind is like the lens of a camera.
If the glass is clear and unclouded,
whatever we see and create will be true.
When the lens of the mind is distorted
by unresolved wants and needs,
we cannot perceive what is true.
Therefore, we cannot create what
is needed. Our work is to calm and
cleanse the mind so that the light
might reach us and flow through
us unencumbered.

Intelligence

The intelligence that could fathom
 a molecule, a moon, water, or sound,
is the same intelligence that lives in you.
Invite your daemon, your genius,
your gift, to come. Believe in its coming.
There is more wisdom in you than
ever you can imagine. We are awareness
itself. We are made of consciousness.
We are one with the Intelligence
that fashioned the stars.

REMOVE THE CLOUDS

There is great value in stilling the body, emotions and mind. We quiet the internal energies to access the wisdom at the root of our own nature. Remembering slowly emerges through our ongoing commitment to remove false ideas and behavioral patterns that keep us from seeing clearly. When we remove the clouds that blind our sight, we feel we are learning something new. But this awareness that dawns on us is not, in fact, new. It is simply accessed through awakening our own deep remembering. As we learn to stabilize and calm our internal energies, we become able to entrain with the strands of consciousness that flow through, in and around us. When this merging occurs, we see and come into alignment with the interconnection of all things. This process cannot be forced. All we can do is remove the energetic turbulence that stands in the way of our remembering.

Transitory Mists

Like clouds floating overhead, our thoughts
and feelings eventually dissolve. When we
recognize them as transitory mists that pass
over the present moment, the world itself
becomes filled with peace. We need to realize
that we are not our thoughts and feelings.
They are fleeting. We are eternal.
When we are able to watch them while
we feel and think them, we become free.

Let Go of Denial

One of the great dangers on the path
to Self-Realization is denial. We not only
deny those areas of dysfunction that are painful
for us to face, we also deny the gifts and abilities
that are a part of us. By so doing we thwart
our growth, limit our potential and hinder
our relationship with Life. The truth that sets
us free is not the grand Cosmic Truth. It is the
small truths we face, or do not face, every day,
moment by moment. There are aspects of self
that need healing. There are qualities that need
to be honored. Let go of the need to deny them.

Unfolding

The important virtues are only learned
with much repetition. Their importance is
revealed again and again in obvious and
then gradually subtler ways. Some of the
deepest virtues, like patience and temperance,
perseverance and compassion, take a lifetime
to assimilate. So relax. The journey is meant
to be a gradual unfolding.

Limited Thoughts

Thoughts are like panes of glass,
lenses through which we view reality.
The glass keeps us from experiencing life
as it truly is. We look through the window
and see the elements moving outside,
but we do not feel their touch. We are
separated from what is. Limited thoughts
give us a false impression of what is true.
Yet when we step outside, allowing our
thoughts to still and our mind to open,
we transcend the confines of our cage of bones.
We are drawn into the vast and glorious silence
of our true Eternal Nature.

SPIRITUAL MATURITY

We may possess much knowledge,
but if we cannot use that knowledge
for the benefit of all, of what value
is it? We may have great wisdom,
but if that wisdom has not seeped
like nourishing rain into the soil of
our thoughts, words and deeds,
what good does it do? We may do
good works, but if those good works
are done for vanity or prestige, do they
ultimately bring joy, balance or peace?
Our spiritual maturity can only be
measured by the thoughts and actions
expressed in our daily lives.

THE SAME ENERGY

When we see one thing as more sacred
than another, we create conflict.
A stone, a cat, a star, a tree, a sinner,
a saint, all carry the same Life Force,
the same Energy that is the Source of all things.
Learn to love and honor all of Creation.
Only then will our petty opinions cease from
creating division, disrespect, negative judgment,
fanaticism and war.

The Path to Fulfillment

Faith is not the belief that only good
will come our way; faith is the certainty
that *all things work together for good.*
If our desire is in alignment with
the right and natural flow of Nature,
miracles occur to bring that desire to fruition.
No matter what events may come our way,
once an aligned intention is created, we remain
quietly confident that life is working its magic.
Every obstacle, disappointment or setback
is an essential stepping-stone along the
path toward fulfillment.

Revolution of Spirit

We live as though we were not in danger
of extinction. In one moment of madness,
the world as we know it could be gone.
We must arise. We must rekindle our
wakefulness. We must passionately
and deliberately offer our hands and
hearts to the great Revolution of Spirit
that must happen now if we are to continue.

Reverie and Activity

The mind is ever over-active.
Our ability to rest and listen lies
buried under a life of fast-paced
activity. When the mind is on
constant output, the emotions
begin to wither. Take time to float,
to dream, to allow days to pass in
aimless reverie. Once reverie and
activity come into harmony,
stress begins to unwind.

Everything is A Teaching

Let every moment be a teaching.
The birds, animals, plants, each have
qualities and gifts that we can learn from.
Observe and be an eternal student of all
that comes your way. Honor everyone
and everything for the lesson they bring
simply by being who they are. A wise person
can reveal a truth that will serve you.
A foolish person can show you the pitfalls
you must avoid. There is wisdom and
folly everywhere. Everything and everyone
is a teaching.

The Worthy Goal

It is possible to be a clear mirror
through which others see a reflection
of their true worth. It is possible to
love others without condition. This only
becomes possible when we no longer
take anything personally, when there is
no need to defend against or blame another,
when there is no desire to teach a lesson
or correct a choice, when we listen carefully
for the full meaning and respond with kindness
and understanding; then unconditional love,
the worthy goal of a lifetime, is blossoming.

Inwardly Yield

Serenity grows out of surrender.
To inwardly yield to life, rather than fight
against its inevitable current, brings peace.
There is great power in surrender.
It does not mean that we never challenge
situations. It means that when we do,
we do it without defensiveness or resistance.
Like water we simply flow around, over,
through or under any obstacle. We swim
the river that appears before us with
an inner serenity and a skillful buoyancy.

The Things that are Small

It is the small things in life that open the heart: the laugh of a child, the beauty of a flower, a simple kindness. Only the present moment can bring joy. There is no peace in striving toward the future. There is no wonder in clinging to the past. In the simplicity of the moment true peace arrives. And when it does, the heart naturally begins to release. Cultivate your love of the things that are small. Watch them. Marvel at them. They are each a doorway into the moment. And the moment is the doorway into the heart.

Inner Stability

When we become overwhelmed by the events and burdens of our life, we can be sure that we are either projecting into the future or ruminating about the past. If we worry about how far we have to go when climbing a mountain, we will falter. But if we place one foot in front of the other, attending to the step we are taking in the present moment, we will eventually take one more step and find ourselves at the top. Our inner stability is found, not in the future or the past, but in being masters of the present moment. The step to follow will always appear once we have tended to the step we are in the process of taking right now.

Small Movement

In those times when our lives seem
to be stagnant, if we listen closely we
might feel an urge, a hunger trying
to speak. Perhaps we long to let go
of a relationship or to change our work.
Perhaps we yearn to begin a spiritual
practice. Perhaps we desire to improve
our diet, change a pattern of behavior
or study something new. If we are
patient and allow hunger to grow,
it will eventually reveal what it is that
is wanting to be born, or is needing
to be left behind. One small movement
in a new direction can alter everything.

Mighty Allies

The mind and the emotions are like
wild ponies. They dart this way and that.
It takes patience, love, perseverance and
attention to tame a wild creature. You have
to understand its ways and work to gain
its confidence. You must learn about its
fears and seek to heal them. The mind
and emotions will serve us faithfully
if we offer them our time, attention and
understanding. Once tamed, they become
mighty allies, willing to carry us powerfully
toward our goal.

Awaken for the Whole

A higher vibration of consciousness is seeking to emerge. It is the survival instinct of the planet. Nature knows that if human beings do not evolve to a less dense vibration, She will have to abort Her experiment. So many of our behavioral patterns have become a cancer. We are over-breeding and over-consuming. We are fouling our nest and destroying other living cells that are vital to the whole. As each one of us begins to vibrate at a higher frequency, it is as if one more white corpuscle in the immune system of the planet begins to fight for our healing. What we awaken within ourselves, we awaken for the whole of Creation.

Wisdom

The mind clings to what it has learned. It insists that we must first understand something before we can trust enough to move forward. We must be willing to let go. We must be willing to take with us only what serves for the next step. Understanding is but a momentary rung on a ladder. We step from one rung to the other until finally we leave the ladder behind. In this way, we arrive one day at the place of Wisdom.

SURRENDER

Surrender to Life. Accept that exactly
what is happening at this very moment
is precisely perfect. It may not be as we
would wish, but it is the wheel's inevitable
turning as it moves along the pathway
of our becoming. To truly surrender, fall
into the arms of the moment. Be at peace
with all it brings. This surrender is where
power originates. Surrender is the road
to contentment.

A ROLLING SEA

It is wise to accept the cyclical flow of things,
for life is a rolling sea. Like the moon, we wax
and wane, like the tides we rise and fall.
When we fully accept that this is the right
and good way of it, we learn to sail our boat
with skill and an open heart.

TRANSFORMED THROUGH TIME

Every step along the pathway of becoming whole requires time.
The body, being composed of a denser vibration, must slowly adjust
to the influx of new energies. Just as an electric wire must be upgraded
for a stronger current to pass through, so must our body be transformed
through time to contain a higher vibration of consciousness.

A Willing Heart

Cultivate cheerfulness. Every day there are
events we may find tedious or stressful.
Let them go. Enter the moment with
a grateful, cheerful attitude, and all manner
of energy and pleasure becomes available
to the mind and body. Happiness does
not begin outside of our self. It is cultivated
from within. No matter the circumstance,
meet it with a willing heart and eventually
joy will blossom.

Radiance

Within the clear light of a crystal
lie all the colors of the rainbow.
Within our own nature lies everything
we need to find our way through the
experiences of this world. Most of us
only use one or two colors. We forget
that we have all the wisdom, strength,
patience, compassion, perseverance,
and joy necessary to meet our every
challenge. Radiance will shine forth
from within when we open to the
Radiant Light that is our True Nature.

Stay Awake and Aware

It takes great tenacity, patience and
vigilance to heal our lives and mature
into our full potential. Every event
that causes anxiety, upset or a reactionary
emotion becomes fertile soil for learning.
Every person with whom we cannot speak
openly and honestly, becomes a teacher.
Each points a way through our fears and
insecurities, back to our essential wholeness.
It takes a daily, ongoing commitment to stay
awake and aware of the areas that are out
of harmony with our highest intent.

Beauty

Let everything we do be done
for Beauty: how we keep our rooms,
tend our garden, or prepare our food.
They say the Spirits love Beauty.
Let Beauty become your mantra
and your devotion. Your inner life
will bloom. Synchronicity will
frequent your door. Wild creatures
will come to call. And your own
heart will grow bright and full
with the same Beauty that you adore.

QUALITIES BLOOM

We cannot force wisdom or understanding to come. We cannot force
the capacity for unconditional love toward all beings to blossom. These
qualities bloom when their season arrives. We can water them with our
attention and with our intention. We can weed away all those qualities that
crowd and stifle their growth. We can cultivate the soil around them and
add fresh nourishment to encourage them to flower. We can quicken and
strengthen them, but we must also learn to wait. Virtues have a wisdom
and timing of their own. They will surely bloom when their time comes.

CREATIVE THOUGHTS

Inspiration is a creative force that
permeates our awareness like breath
permeates the molecules of the body.
We become infused, filled with the
thoughts upon which we dwell.
Our creative thoughts become
the dreams that set the intentions
that guide our lives. Watch carefully.
The thoughts that excite you, be they
beautiful or gross, become the pathway
you are laying out before you. You will
have to walk this path. Be sure that
you are creating the journey you truly
desire to take.

BE A QUIET HARBOR

You cannot know where the pains
and tragedies of life are leading.
Sorrow is always near, whether it
is touching you personally at this
moment or not. Cultivate tenderness
for all beings. The drama in which
they may be trapped at the moment
is the same as you have experienced
in the past, or will experience in the
future. Be a quiet and peaceful harbor
for whoever might need you.

Meet Each Moment

No matter what circumstance
may come your way, judge it as
neither good nor bad. Remember,
life is a process. Allow it to be,
for this moment, exactly what it is.
It will change. We can never know
the intricate workings of life, nor can
we know where any situation will lead.
Our responsibility is to meet each
moment as a true spiritual warrior:
alert and prepared. Every moment offers
one more opportunity to hold steady.
This is how we practice Self-Mastery.

Transformation

Rather than calling down Creation
to fulfill our needs and desires, we must
uplift our needs and desires so that
Creation itself may be fulfilled.
Our only work is to transform base
metals, our thoughts and feelings,
into gold. Our daily lives have no ultimate
purpose other than this great alchemical
transformation of being. Every moment
offers an opportunity to surrender to
the great work of maturing humanity
by expanding our own consciousness
and leading evolution onward.

STEP THROUGH

There are moments throughout our lives
when we arrive at a doorway, a choice point.
If we fail to see the moment for what it is,
we may have to wait years to arrive at another
such opportunity. Be ever vigilant. Do not
overlook the doorway into transformation
when it arrives. And do not, for fear of the
risk, miss the chance to step through that door.

Conscious and Aware

All of nature is comprised of strands
of light, energy that in itself is conscious
and aware. Consciousness is the very
building block of all that exists in the
world of form. Our body is composed
of interconnecting filaments of awareness.
Because we are made of consciousness itself,
we can become conscious of an endless sea
of knowledge that is presently hidden
from us. The act of awakening is simply
the act of remembering this knowledge
that has been forgotten. Our duty is to
do all we can to stimulate and activate
our ability to remember.

Learn to Store Energy

To live the impeccable life we must learn
to store energy. We waste an enormous
amount of life force through indulging
emotionally and mentally. We allow the
mind and emotions to remain completely
undisciplined. We lose control of the
perception through which we experience
the world. Once we learn to steady the
mind and emotions through remaining
awake in the present moment, then we
will hold the life force needed to penetrate
into deeper awareness.

COMMITTED AND SURRENDERED

When we couple our masculine capacity
to be clear and decisive, with our feminine
ability to wholeheartedly receive, faith
resonates strongly enough to do its work.
Faith is born of mental clarity and conviction
as well as emotional gratitude and assurance.
The more energy and consciousness we
activate, the more we are able to manifest
our heart's desire. We can cultivate our
ability to be actively clear and committed,
while remaining passively surrendered and sure.

DETACHMENT

We become truly compassionate
when we are wise enough to remain
inwardly detached from the melodrama
of life. True detachment is the ability
to allow everything and everyone,
to be where they are and who they are.
It is an ability to remain centered
and grounded whether our advice
or offering is received or rejected.
Detachment is not indifference to the
feelings or suffering of others. It is the
quiet understanding that everything
is unfolding exactly as it should.

INNER CHANGE

Every thought, word and deed
is a pebble in a pool. The ripples
circle outward. They eventually
reach the shore and then return to us.
We are the creators of the life we are living.
If we do not like our present circumstance,
we have only to look within to see the
choices we have made that have brought
us here. Only through inner change
can we hope to transform our external
experience. The work always lies within.

LAYERS OF REALITY

The body is not only a vessel that
carries us through this world, it is also
a vehicle into realms we cannot even
imagine. Our body offers us an opportunity
to travel through varied layers of reality.
The great gift of a human life is the chance
to explore through emotion, feeling, thought,
sensation, activity, dream and stillness.
Sink into your body, journey into its depths.
Just as there is a universe outside of us that
reaches beyond the stars, so is there a universe
within, that is even more vast and unfathomable.

The Fire of Truth

The journey toward Self-Realization is not always comfortable.
The more knowledge we possess, the more we are held accountable.
The nearer the light, the sharper and more pronounced the shadow.
Self-Realization involves a burning away of all those beliefs, behaviors
and reactions that are not aligned with the Higher Good. The closer
we draw to the fire of truth the hotter the flame becomes. Use this
added heat and clarity to quicken your own becoming.

SHED WHAT BELONGS TO THE PAST

There are times when we have outgrown
a situation, when there is no further nurture
to be gained. This is the moment we must be
willing to let go. For like the serpent whose skin
has grown too tight and worn, we need to shed
what belongs to the past to move into the new
possibility. We may feel vulnerable for a time,
but greater ease of movement will assuredly come.

WHEN TO LET GO

Just as geese know the time and season
to begin their journey, so will our instincts
sense when we are ready to transform that
which no longer serves. It takes courage
to risk movement. If we tarry too long
we may miss the window of opportunity
and fall prey to the winter's cold. Listen to
your inner knowing. It will tell you when to
let go, when to risk and when to step forward.

The Urge of Evolution

The great souls of this world offer a glimpse
of the magnificent potential that lies
dormant within each one of us. They are
the way-showers, the urge of evolution
revealed. Learn from them, whatever
their religion or philosophy. Throw open
the windows. Unlock the doors. Become
a student of all that is beautiful and true,
no matter what outer garment it may wear.

Gems

Think of the joys and sorrows
of your life as gems of varying hues.
Some may be dark while others sparkle.
When strung together they make up
the unique design of your life. Most
gems are forged through great pressure.
Most lives have known great stress and
strain. Let the pressures that you have
endured transform you into a luminous
being, refracting from each experience
a reflection of great beauty.

Our Own True Nature

We can never be separated from that for which we seek. The Great Mystery permeates all things, seen and unseen. It may be difficult to grasp that the Mystery, which is our essential Self, is the same Mystery that fashioned the stars. But once we experience our bodies as being one with the Universe, and know this to be so, we know our own true Nature for the first time.

SACRIFICING RESISTANCE

SACRIFICE ALL YOUR RESISTANCE

We are turning base metals into gold.
We are transforming ourselves so a new era
for humanity can begin. We are surrendering
our separateness so we can harmonize once
more with Creation. The time for this
work is now. Now, before it is too late.
Give everything you have to this great
awakening. Sacrifice all your resistance
upon the altar of your own becoming.
Nothing less will do.

ALLOW THE SELF TO EMERGE

Do not ask for God to come to you.
Allow the Self, the vast Mystery,
to emerge from the depth of your own
Being. Recognize that you have never,
in anything but your own mind, been
separate or apart from this Mystery.
Identify your Self as being one with
the Creator. This is what we call
Self-Realization.

SIMPLE

The ruminations of the mind shut out
the simple truths of life. Be present
to everything, the nuance of color,
the scent of rose, the touch of a
breeze, the sound of a bird. These
simple pleasures can bring such joy.
Complexity is a trap of the mind.
That which is most precious and
true is always simple.

THE DAWN

As a moth is drawn inevitably toward
the light, so are we drawn inevitably
toward ever-brighter illumination and
awareness. Every moment of every day
brings experience that will eventually
lead to greater understanding. There is
no rush, no time limit, no ultimate danger.
A moment comes for every person when
the dawn begins to break. When it does,
we will move toward that light instinctively.
It is in our nature to do so.

WHOLENESS

One by one the body centers become
activated. We become more stable, more
flexible, more attuned. As the emotions
become tamed and the mind grows quiet,
a whole new life begins to emerge. One part
of the self no longer fights with the other.
We become balanced and whole. There is
harmony. This gradual unfolding toward
wholeness, in the end, flowers as joy.

ALIGN WITH ESSENCE

We are one with the Force that fashioned
Creation. That which created All That Is
flows through us as our essential Self.
We have but to align with this essence
for our life to be transformed. This
awakening to who we actually are is
why we are here. It is our birthright
and our gift. It may take lifetimes for
this to become fully realized, but what
greater gift can we ever give or receive?

Enlivening Energy

As the body, mind and emotions become
more integrated, our true Self begins
to emerge. We realize that we are not
separate and apart from the world.
We are actually one with it. The same
enlivening energy that flows through
us flows through all things. Like the
stones, stars and oceans, we are patterns
of energy composed of the one unifying
Essence that permeates all things.

Cycles of Renewal

We resurrect ourselves again and again.
Dreams rise and fall and rise again,
only to fall. We let them die that they
may be born anew in a finer form.
Always after loss there is a perfect
interlude that will allow a regeneration
to occur. When the dark night is past,
unexpectedly, yet right on time, the light
returns and we are resurrected, reborn,
renewed. Allow for the cycles of renewal.
Spring always returns.

HIDDEN TEACHERS

It is not only in the relative world that it can be said, *when the student is ready, the master will come.* There are hidden teachers who walk with us. There are ancestors who wait to support us, spirits whose work it is to help us. Call this support what you will: angels, guides, the Higher Self, the Holy Spirit. That which we need is with us at all times. Wc can sense the Presence through our intuition. We have but to be still, listen and hear.

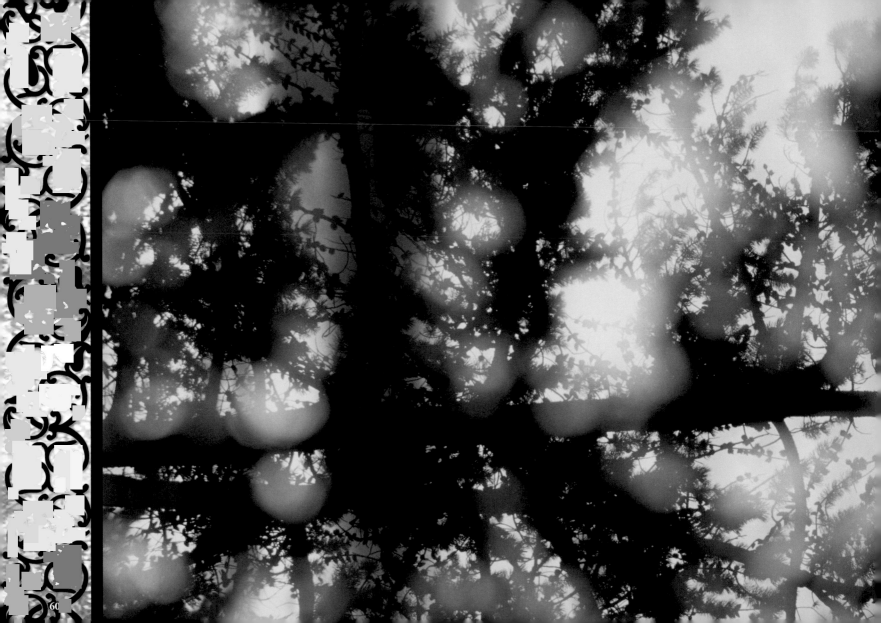

Living Vital Force

There is a vibrating, radiant force that energizes and connects us with the source of all creation. It is the energy of which our own body is composed. We vibrate with the same life that vibrates the waters, the earth and the stars. All is connected in this living vital force. All is motivated and sustained by its power. Realize this. Take responsibility for being the co-creator of your life.

REPROGRAM

We must reprogram all of the emotional
and mental habits that no longer serve.
What we feel and think determines
our future in more ways than we can
imagine. The energies of our body align
with our thoughts and feelings to create
a pathway of expectation ahead of us,
for better or ill. Be ever vigilant.
Observe yourself. See that your
Higher Self, and nothing else,
is the conscious creator of the path
you wish to tread.

HUMILITY

Feelings of doubt or inadequacy,
rather than being a source of shame,
can become a simple reminder of the
value of humility. There will always
be more to know, to understand
and experience. Even our conceived
inadequacies are perfectly appropriate
for the moment in which we find
ourselves. Do not let the awareness
of the path yet untraveled blind you
to the gifts that are alive in you right
now. A small sapling in the forest is
no less perfect than the mighty cedar
standing tall.

PERFECTION

Let go of false ideas about perfection.
Perfection is not a state to be realized
somewhere in the future. It exists here
and now. Even what appears to be
a mistake offers a stepping-stone toward
greater wisdom. My flaw may be your
opportunity. We are at different places
along the pathway of unfolding.
Every mistake offers the possibility
for awakening. Every awakening could
potentially lead to our next mistake.
Our life proceeds from possibility to
possibility, from mistake to mistake,
or from awakening to awakening.
It all depends on our point of view.

THE HIDDEN CORRIDORS

The personal ego, until it has been tamed,
is always saying, 'Look at me,' or perhaps,
'Don't look at me'. It all depends on how
the ego has reacted to the essential wound
it carries. To heal the ego's need to brag
or to whine we must make the descent
into the hidden hallways of the psyche,
where knowledge of the small self dwells.
But as we explore our past wounds, we must
be sure to also ascend into alignment with
the Higher Self. The Soul Self is detached
enough to shine a clear, honest light even
into our darkest corridors.

SHAME

Shame is debilitating. Its only
purpose is to shock us momentarily
when we have behaved with unconscious
inappropriateness. To be ashamed
in order to notice our own folly
is a useful awakener. We must then
see our mistake, put in the correction
and move on. To linger in shame is
self-destructive as well as self-indulgent.
Recognize shame when it arrives.
Learn from it and then banish it
as quickly as you can.

ACCEPTANCE

It takes time to learn acceptance.
The small self desires to be wealthy,
secure, unique, and so much more.
To truly accept the life we have been given,
we must pass through many states of being:
disappointment, hope, sadness, frustration,
excitement, loss. Transformation can only
flower with the acceptance of all life brings.
After a long journey, we finally see that the
life we are living is simply what it is:
the life that we are living.

EMPTY

Like the cycles of the moon, every phase
has its purpose, its moment and its demise.
We must allow the cup to empty when
it is time. Once empty, the virtue of
patience, so difficult to embrace, will
gradually wear down our resistance to
life as it is. Only then will we fill with
new and fresh waters. And surrender,
the final devotion, will rise.

MASTERY

We are meant to struggle and to thereby
grow strong. Strength and courage are
born out of our perseverance in the face
of suffering and discouragement. It takes
great determination to awaken from our
self-absorption. Cynicism, resignation and
hopelessness: each is a form of resistance
to life being the way that it is. As we mature
in mastery, the resistance transforms.
We experience more acceptance and ease
in place of struggle and disappointment.

NON-JUDGMENT

When we judge others, we judge ourselves. When we judge ourselves, we find
that we also judge others. The person who has no need to place himself above
or below anyone is truly free. Watch for the subtle pleasure you experience
when you feel superior to another. Uncover the narcissistic self-pity you
experience when you feel less than another. Search deeply to find the arrogance
that needs to look down upon or belittle either your own self or someone else.
It is the ego alone that judges. We all struggle, at one time or another,
with the self-same lessons that must eventually be learned. Learn the lesson
of non-judgment now and a new peace will find its way to your door.

TEMPERANCE

When a sword is tempered, it is first heated to melting point then hammered into a desired shape. It is plunged into cold water. Once cooled, it is fired and hammered again until it grows sharp and strong. This tempering makes the sword worthy of being carried by a king. As we learn to endure and surrender to the fire, the hammer, and the cold, we grow strong and uncomplaining. We are able to face whatever comes, holding our temper, while we ourselves are being tempered. We accept the paradox of joy and sorrow, justice and injustice, abundance and scarcity with true temperance and grace. Temperance is our ability to endure with sobriety and equanimity the transforming fires of experience and the dowsing waters of disappointment. Temperance is the ability to allow ourselves to be molded into the being we are intended to be.

WISDOM

The same world is very different to
each one of us. We are able to see and
appreciate only to the degree to which
we have mastered our mind and emotions.
Our work is to tune our thoughts and
feelings to become so stable, and yet
so flexible, that Life will reveal to us
Her deeper mysteries. Wisdom is not
wasted on the self-indulgent. Wisdom
is the reward of the steadfast moment-
by-moment discipline and perseverance
of the one who aspires.

SELF-DISCIPLINE

Self-discipline is the commitment to disciple
ourselves to the highest we can perceive.
It takes enormous energy to hold fast to
a commitment once it has been made.
Those who keep their word create
an accountability toward which
ever-greater energy begins to flow.
Those who remain mindful and have
the impeccable patience to complete
the work at hand, gain the stability
and sobriety required to fulfill the journey.

MEET EVERY MOMENT

When we lose our self-pity, a whole
new world opens. We often act as if life
has singled us out to cause us personal
struggle. But life is simply life. We either
face what comes to us with courage and
forbearance, or we fall into complaining
and feeling sorry for ourselves. To meet
every moment as a challenge is the only
way to find peace. When we are content
with what is, even a setback becomes
a doorway.

COSMIC TIMING

We cannot know the appropriate timing
for events to occur in our lives. There is
a hidden perfection that orchestrates all things.
Learn to accept and surrender to the mystery
of Cosmic Timing. Allow anxiety to transform
into patience. Allow disappointment to become
quiet perseverance. Allow loneliness to evolve
into fulfilled aloneness. It is through building
strength by facing opposition that the great
virtues are born.

CRISIS

Crisis is a doorway to greater understanding
and harmony. Without crisis to inform
us of disharmony, we may tarry too
long and lose the chance to transform.
When crisis arrives, do not fight it.
Become alert. Seek the source of the
imbalance and correct it. Crisis is a truth
serum. Learn from it and harmony
will be restored. Ignore it, and greater
sorrow is to follow.

APPRECIATION

Appreciation is a combination of honor
and gratitude. Everything thrives on
appreciation. As often as possible,
offer your appreciation. Express it openly.
Give it freely, whether to a stranger,
a loved one, an animal or a rose.
Appreciation refreshes and uplifts a
person who is disheartened or a society
that has lost its way. Let small acts
of kindness and appreciation kindle
light wherever you go.

DENIAL

It takes many, many years to integrate
the personality. What we believe and
experience is often distorted by layers
of denial. The need to avoid unpleasant
truths about the self by falsely interpreting
reality is a danger that is always with us.
Denial is a most difficult hurdle to
overcome. Yet, the ability to face reality
with an unflinching eye is the mark of
the true spiritual warrior.

PRECIOUS ENERGY

An unwanted habit that is maintained
for too long weakens the spirit. Each time
you betray yourself by doing what you
wish not to do or not doing what you
wish to do, you leak precious energy that
is needed for the journey of evolution.
Our energy field is like a thin porcelain bowl.
If there are cracks that form, we must act
to re-seal them. Each of us is given our
allotment of life force at birth. We must
guard it lest we find ourselves too weakened
to hold our dreams.

Inspiration

Why wait for inspiration to come?
Inspiration may or may not arrive.
If it does, it will only come periodically
on the winds of chance. But if we court
inspiration by setting time aside, if we
create an atmosphere of expectancy,
inspiration will find us irresistible
and will come often. If you desire
to be inspired, set time aside, make
yourself ready, and wait. Slowly a
powerful relationship between you and
Spirit, the Source of All Inspiration,
will arise.

Give Thanks

Gratitude opens the heart to joy.
Thank you for the loss that deepens me.
Thank you for the sorrow that humbles me.
Thank you for the pain that tempers me,
the work that strengthens me, the
disappointments that help me to surrender.
Thank you for the changing fortunes of life
that teach discernment, compassion,
perseverance, patience, courage and so much
more. We either give thanks for all that comes
our way, even if it causes us to weep, or we
remain small, petty and complaining.

LAYER AFTER LAYER

The ego is a master deceiver. It tricks us into believing all manner of confusing nonsense. The minute we become aware that our beliefs or actions are no longer serving us, the ego shifts its point of view and we become ensnared in a more subtle delusion. Layer after layer of camouflage must be removed. Finally we reach the fear that is at the root of all the maneuvers the ego employs to avoid its feeling of insecurity: the fear that we are nothing, the fear that we are not separate and more special than others. The fear that we will die and be forgotten. When we face and accept that what we most fear is, in fact, the Truth, we may simply laugh out loud and move into freedom.

Patience and Courage

Somewhere within we always know if we are on the right path or not. We may not know where we are meant to go or what we need to do, but we always know if we are truly at peace with the choices we are making. We race from activity to activity, from relationship to relationship, frantically trying to pacify the inner disturbance. And yet, in times of transition what we need is patience and courage. Courage to admit when we are off course, patience to stop and wait for an insight to reveal where our next step should be, and then courage to follow that guidance. Change is best served with patience and courage.

UNCONDITIONAL AND FREE

Love is not a feeling; it is a state of being that you enter after a long, long journey. When fear no longer dictates our response to that which threatens, when the sword is laid down, and the cup is truly empty, having been drunk to the last drop, when there is no more dishonoring, and our peevish opinions about what anyone or anything should be fall away, then we can step through the door. The world is forever altered. What we once thought to be love is seen for what it was, a hunger and a need. And true love, unconditional and free, dawns like the sun within us. Love, the Great Includer, begins to shine.

Vaster Being

A hunger for recognition is a primary
dysfunction of the small ego. Like a needy
child, the ego does not yet realize who it is.
We become so identified with our passing
personality that we forget we are a much
vaster being. We are an infinite essence
having the experience of a finite adventure.
If you remember yourself at five or six years
old, where is that boy or girl now? Childhood
has already become but a remembered dream.
Once we open to who we really are, our small
self with its petty upsets and its need for
recognition fades and dissolves. We see
our passing life for what it is: a fleeting,
momentary dream.

Grace

Grace is undying favor, the unexpected balm
of the Unknowable. Like the air we breathe,
grace flows through, around and in everything.
We have only to sink into the deep resonance
of this very moment now to receive its blessing.
Grace is always present, waiting to bestow its
healing breath upon whoever draws near.
It is we who must approach in the stillness.
It is we who must open to receive. Grace is
a constant. We are the variable. The more
constant our surrender, the more grace-filled
we become.

CULTIVATE COURAGE

Fear is both a protector and an adversary.
Our fears of what others will say, of where
our livelihood will come from, of whether
we are adequate for the task weaken us.
We forfeit the true journey of Self-Realization
by succumbing to these fears. Cultivate courage
and the ability to listen to the inner voice.
Hold true to that knowing regardless of
the fears that may arise. Fear in one form
or another will be a constant companion
through life. It is a part of our protective shield.
We must, therefore, balance it always with
an equal portion of courage.

BLESSING

To the degree that we are able to empty ourselves
of resistance to life as it is in this moment,
to that degree we are available to recognize
and receive blessing. For every moment
contains a gift. It might be the gift of patience,
perseverance or surrender. It might be the
gift of endurance or compassion. The blessing
is always available to those who can receive.

COMPLAINING

Any form of complaining is the small self becoming lost in self-importance. So much energy needed for awakening is wasted on complaining. We may not be able to change our external reality, but we can transform the negative thoughts and feelings that are our reaction to that reality. We have a chance to awaken from the nightmare we create through our resistance to what is. Stopping all complaining is one of the first steps. When we cease to complain, we conserve life force for what really matters. A new world begins. Each event becomes a mysterious opportunity rather than an inconvenient vexation. A tremendous amount of life force, once bound up in feeling sorry for oneself, is released. Where once there was frustration and self-pity, there is now space for appreciation to bloom. The misguided belief that life should be other than it is dissolves and in its place, acceptance flowers, joy awakens, patience blossoms, and peace permeates.

Consciousness

We are trapped by what we are capable of perceiving as much as by
what we are incapable of knowing. We are imprisoned by our need
to believe that what we perceive is all that can be perceived. There
are other dimensions and other worlds that exist beyond our senses.
To experience these worlds, we must learn to expand our consciousness.
Meditation, ritual, shamanic journeys, prayer, trance dancing, dreaming
and contemplating are a few of the tools that can assist us as we open to
these higher states of consciousness. It is arrogance and ignorance that
reduces life to be but the world we believe in or see around us.

VULNERABILITY

There is grace and beauty in vulnerability:
the fragility of a petal, the tenderness of
a baby, the delicacy of a heart opening to
speak. True intimacy arrives with vulnerability.
We cannot receive another until we lay down
our defensive shield. We cannot give of our
true self until we throw down the sword.
It is a privilege of the highest order to be
allowed to glimpse the Holy of Holies within
another. There is no greater gift of trust than
to be openly vulnerable.

LEARN THE LANGUAGE

Every plant and animal carries an essential
vibration and quality that can assist us on
our journey. Become watchful. Observe
everything as it comes and goes throughout
the day. Life is speaking to us directly
through indirect means. Learn the language
of the world we are living in. Become adept
at translating the signs that appear. There is
guidance coming to us from the deep
conscious realms of creation.

BENEVOLENCE TO ALL

It has been said that the sun rises on
the evildoer as well as upon the virtuous.
And just so, develop your own nature
to give benevolence to all. It is not ours
to judge who is worthy and who is not.
We can never know the undercurrents
that are working out their alchemy in the
heart of another. You would not discredit
a child for being young, so why judge
anyone for being at the stage of development
they happen to be. Cultivate compassionate
discernment in a neutral kindly heart.

A PASSING STEP

Forgiveness is a passing step upon the journey
toward true understanding. There comes
a time when we realize that all of us are
ultimately blameless for our wrong-doings.
We are victims of our own unconsciousness.
Forgiveness helps us to release our judgment
of self, as well as others, so that acceptance,
compassion and understanding can be born
within us. In the end, there is no ultimate
need to forgive.

CHARACTER

The purpose of activity is not the
accomplishment itself, but the character
that is developed during the activity.
If you find yourself in a period of inactivity,
continue to develop character. It is not
what we do, but the quality with which
we do it that is our accomplishment.
We must beware of judging ourselves
by our activity. Better to value the peace
and emotional stability that accompanies
our actions. These things endure.

DISAPPOINTMENTS

Disappointments only arrive when we
have a preconceived idea of how our
lives should unfold. Often the thing we
thought to be a devastating blow turns
out to be a great gift. Our disappointments
hollow us out. They test, humble, educate
and move us. Ease and pleasure do not
prod us on to evolve. It is our frustrations
and sorrows that, like the grit in the oyster,
fashion thc pcarl of our becoming.

PRAY UNCEASINGLY

Pray unceasingly that all denial be
stripped from your mind. Pray that
something miraculous be born within
us all. Give everything you have.
Do not wait another day. Lay your
hours and intellect, your heart
and passion, upon the altar of
self-transformation and collective
awakening. Begin now: pray,
believe, trust and act.

CLEAR PERSPECTIVE

All we need in order to evolve exists
in this present moment now. Why do
we fight the circumstances that are
happening in our lives? We cannot
redirect our path until we are able to
see and honestly accept the place in
which we find ourselves. Once we
have a clear perspective of where we
actually are, we will know how to step
wisely in the direction we need to go.

Volatile Vessel

The body is a volatile vessel, sailing effortlessly
one moment, shipwrecked the next. Become
a skilled sailor so you can navigate this life.
Cultivate such a capacity to be present in the
moment that no sudden change of weather
can overthrow your presence of mind. It is only
when we are fully centered that we can respond
swiftly to the coming of a storm. The ship's
captain always knows how to respond when his
vessel is blown off course. He remains stable and
flexible regardless of the circumstance. The need
for correction becomes second nature when we
have mastered the body, mind and emotion.

The Drama of Life

Those who have committed themselves
to vigilantly observe their own reactions
to the ups and downs of experience are
those who eventually master the role they
have been called upon to play. Most of us
are too lost in the drama of life to ever step
back and rewrite the script we are living.
If we do not like the content of a scene
we are enacting, we can choose to change
it. We each are the author, director and actor
in the play that is unfolding. But only
through constant vigilance can we become
sensitive and astute enough to know what
in the plot needs to be changed.

IDENTIFY WITH NOTHING

The thoughts and beliefs with which
we identify hold the smaller self captive.
We identify with being good or bad, weak
or strong. We believe our worth lies in
whether we are wealthy, beautiful, intelligent,
famous, married, successful or some other
self-imposed value. And when the relationship
is over or the money is gone, when beauty
fades, when the pretense is revealed or the
position is lost, we no longer know who
we are. Identify with nothing. Everything
is made of smoke. In the end, it is only our
essential nature that remains.

BALANCE

The compulsive habit that causes us to lose
ourselves in a maze of unhappiness is always
with us. It takes great vigilance to become
adept enough to notice the moment we are
being mesmerized by thoughts and feelings
that ensnare. Every day, moment by moment,
we can learn to recognize when we are being
lured into identifying with life as a melodrama.
This does not mean we lose our ability to feel.
Rather, we gain an ability to catch ourselves
before we fall. We say, 'There I go again.'
And the instant we become aware that we are
falling, we become able to regain our balance.

ENDLESS BECOMING

Do not be afraid or over-anxious about time.
Time is like water, lapping against stone.
Patiently, day by day, it removes and reshapes,
one speck at a time. And as surely as water
gradually reworks stone, we too are reshaped
by Time. There is no rush. We have an eternity
to experience. We are not fixed. We are an
endless Becoming. The more we yield to
the transformation that Time inevitably
brings, the easier life becomes. Patience is
the ability to face this endless chipping away,
this ceaseless Becoming, with equanimity
and a detached, accepting surrender.

BRING DOWN THE SWORD

All anger is fear and helplessness in disguise.
We cannot hold the tragedies, disappointments
and heartbreaks of life. In our weakness,
we thrash and blame. We refuse to accept.
We waste our precious life force on emotional
histrionics. Tragedy and injustice will be with
us always. When we acknowledge that we are
helpless to change this fact, when we accept
that it is neither good nor bad that life is so,
then freedom from anger arrives. We become
able to face life as it is and to speak our truth
clearly. We can then bring down the sword
when necessary without any debilitating loss
of inner stability.

PECULIAR PERFECTION

When we are at peace with our own nature we never need to pretend to be more or less than we are. Self-righteousness is an expression of inner uncertainty. Arrogance expresses a fear of inadequacy. When confronted with our inabilities, we can either learn something new about ourselves, or we can deny, distort and pretend. We are pieces in a jigsaw puzzle. We fit perfectly, exactly as we are, into the space that has been prepared for us. Any smaller or any larger space will not do. The picture of life would not be complete if any one of us were different than we are at this time, in this moment. It is a peculiar perfection.

Spring Appears

Just when you think the winter will never cease, suddenly spring appears.
So it is with sadness, sorrow, loneliness or loss. Everything has its day and
its season. A new bud will appear where a barren twig lay empty. A fresh
start will burst forth with the first green leaf. An unexpected possibility,
a new life, will be felt among the ruins. Have faith. Expect the impossible.
Trust the unfolding nature of life. Wait an eternity if need be. Spring,
inevitable, will surely come.

Support

Just as rain and sun and moon and water support a plant to grow, so there are beings, both seen and unseen, whose work it is to support our unfolding. It is the imperative of all Creation to aid evolution. When we align with life and swim with the current, when we do not resist its flow, all manner of unexpected forces arise to direct our course. We are never alone in our awakening. To all the unseen forces who support us, our awakening is a joy.

Step Forward

Our attachment to our own story limits our freedom. We cling to the woes of the past as if they justify the present. We limit our potential by remaining devoted to our limiting beliefs. We repeat ourselves endlessly, never realizing that a new road ahead lies waiting. Our creative spirit, our thoughts and feelings decide the pathway forward. Let go of the stepping-stones of the past. Step forward into whatever the moment brings. Allow life to unfold as the adventure it is meant to be.

INTEGRATION

There are many beings living within us –
the child who demands attention, the warrior
with courage to meet circumstance, the victim
full of self pity, the seeker reaching for understanding, the coward unable to face reality.
All these beings vie within us for supremacy.
One by one we must come to know them all.
One by one we must include and integrate
them into our vaster Self. Not one of them
can be ignored or left behind, for each is an
aspect of the whole. Only through integration
can we know true mastery.

MASTERY

Mastery is about inclusion, rather than exclusion.
When we can accept all parts of our nature
without flinching, when we can allow others
and circumstances to be what they are, when we
can receive what life brings without complaint,
then we will have integrated our smaller self into
our Higher Self. It is the work of our Eternal
Nature to include, within its timelessness, the
finite time-bound aspect that we are living now.
This is the Mastery of Self-Realization.

The Tension

Every setback in our life is merely the backward pull of the bow, which creates the tension that will eventually release the arrow. If we can hold the tension, while keeping an eye set firmly upon the goal, our aim will be true and our goal will be reached. Everything contains within it a tension as it is being birthed. The push of a young sprout against the resistance of frozen soil builds stamina and strength for the inevitable emergence of spring. Accept the challenges of life. They move us toward our fulfillment.

Following Spirit

The forces of nature are always working to support our integration. We are being drawn toward wholeness. It is our destiny and our birthright. The Great Attractor is influencing us whether we are aware of it or not. Awakening quickens when we respond to the pull of Creation. Cultivate a deep longing for wholeness, an absolute commitment to self-transformation, an ability to penetrate silence, and a full surrender to following the dictates of Spirit as they arise from within and from without.

DIVINE WILL

Our purpose is not to slay the ego, but to absorb it completely into the fullness of our true Being. The ego or finite self must eventually become one with the Higher, Infinite Self. It is only then that we can be led by the Will of Heaven rather than by the petty demands of personal preferences. When we anchor our consciousness in the belly, we are literally bringing Heaven to Earth. The ego, which is so often motivated by insecurity, relaxes. As the ego lets go of its need for control, it finds itself at peace and in service to the Divine Will.

THE DREAM OF LIFE

Look back at your childhood. Remember your youth. These memories are like a dream floating among dreams, even though, at the time, they appeared real. When we are gone from this life, we will look back at our time here as a dream among dreams. We have power to influence the dream we are dreaming now. We can awaken and begin to witness the events of our lives as passing phantoms in a mirage. They are real and yet, they are not real. It is never too late. Our life can become the dream we were born to dream.

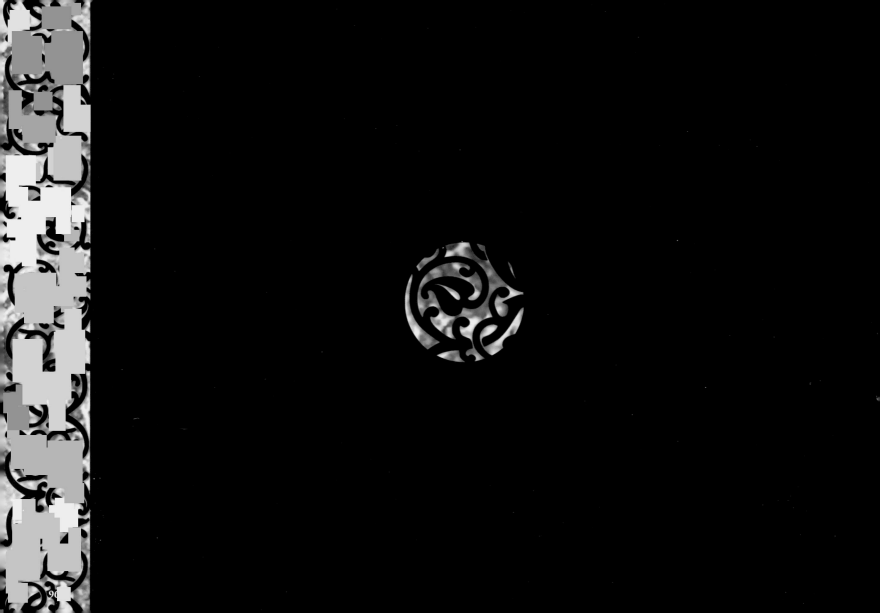

THE LISTENING HEART

THE SUSTAINERS

The plant kingdom is considered to be the kingdom of Healers.
They are the sustainers, the ones who bring nurture and balance.
As we grow in appreciation for their abundant giving, we find
the quality of reverence beginning to awaken in us. Humble
and humus are words that come from the same root. To love
the plants is one of the finest ways to discover humility. To fully
appreciate the plant world, we must bow before them, in awe
of our utter dependence on their generosity.

The Ancient Way

The body holds many secrets. Breath is
a carriage on which we ride to penetrate
the body's hidden mysteries. The ancient
way of following the breath allows us
to enter the silence of the body's inner
sanctuary. Here, within that silence,
subtle feelings and intuitions awaken
and guide us to what is true.

Enter the Sound

Every cell in your body vibrates with
the same vitality that upholds the
universe. Listen deeply. Hear that vibration
singing in your ears. Enter the sound.
It reverberates through the whole of the
body, energizing, enlivening, permeating.
This is the hum of the universe. The life
force sings in every thing. Allow the sound
to dissolve stress, heal dis-ease and vitalize
 every cell.

SIGNS AND SIGNALS

The deepest realms of consciousness communicate to us through the language of symbol, sign and synchronicity. Outer life, like a dream, also speaks through serendipitous events. Our ancestors knew this and depended upon the information they received. Today, more and more of us are remembering how to communicate and receive guidance through such signs and signals. We must awaken our shamanic roots. By so doing we will connect our instinctual knowing with our logical and spiritual understandings so we may move forward.

Our Body

Our body is fashioned to feel the Presence, to intuit the Essence, and to become one with the Animating Principle. When we go inward, a world that is still and potent awakens. This is the threshold through which we must pass to arrive at the transcendent. Through the body of form we are able to gain access to the formless Soul, our connection with that which is beyond all knowing.

An Unknown Reality

We have become trapped in the everyday known universe. We have forgotten that there are unknown realities swirling around and within us, realities that we cannot perceive with our everyday senses. We forfeit wonder and joy when we view the world as obvious and understandable. The world is not understandable. What we see is merely the outer skin of a vast and glorious mystery. When we bow in awe and reverence before that Mystery, an energy is released that causes the Mystery to stir and vibrate in response to our attention.

ENTER THE SILENCE

There is great teaching in the heart of Silence.
Learn to sit without need for thought or action.
Life passes swiftly and in the end, it is what
has awakened within us that will remain.
All actions disappear, all adventures fade.
But wisdom gleaned through reflection
lasts long after life is gone. Allow contemplation
to visit you often and wisdom will become
your companion. Enter the Silence daily
and the Silence will enter you.

ONE WITH ALL

There is a unifying inner current,
a life force that flows in and through
all things. It is this essential and conscious
energy that binds all of life together.
The person we think our self to be
is merely a momentary manifestation
of this ongoing life current. Once we
realize this to be true, our attachment
to our particular personality begins
to weaken. We see ourselves as one
with all things, no more or less important.

A Wise Teacher

When you dive into the silence within
you enter a deep reservoir of wisdom,
love and power. Take time each day to
go within. Meditate upon the silence,
and you will drink the elixir of the gods.
All great souls have cultivated the ability
to hear the inner voice of silence. It is from
here that all new thought, all music, vision
and creativity arise. Approach Silence as
you would approach a wise teacher, with
an open willingness to learn.

Deliberate Steps

After years and years, and even lifetimes,
of slow deliberate steps, the student will
begin to realize the fruits of all his labor.
If we cultivate persistent patience and steadfast
commitment, we will approach the door.
Entrance is only granted to those who have
been purified and grown strong by the slow
and gradual stripping away of the false self.
There is no fast track to awakening.
Patience is a prerequisite.

THE SWORD

When we first set foot upon the path of
awakening, we take a two-edged sword into
our hands. At each turn upon the road,
we must use that sword to clear a pathway
into the unknown. We must also use it to
sever what needs to die within our own lives.
We must be ruthless with all that is false,
misguided or deluded. If we cling to false
ideas and beliefs about our self or the world
around us, the sword will grow heavy in
our hands. We must either drop the sword
and remain in ignorance, or wield the sword
on behalf of the Truth.

NATURE

The more we allow for the changing
circumstances of life, the more stable and
easy we become. There is no greater teacher
than Nature: one moment, a storm, the next,
stillness. If we allow ourselves to listen and
receive when in Her Presence, we will
eventually give birth to balance, patience,
endurance and surrender. By embracing
Her teachings we mature into wisdom.

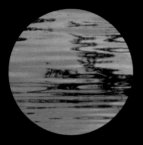

DIVE

The kingfisher is willing to dive from the air into the water in order to catch the silver fish. So must we dive from thought into the silence of the subconscious realms if we wish to discover and be nourished by the treasures that lie within. Attachment to our accustomed thoughts and beliefs can keep us from venturing beyond the conscious mind, into the unknown depth where fresh nurture lies.

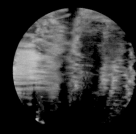

DRINK FROM THE STILLNESS

Dip into the still pool that is always within before beginning
any creative endeavor. Once the conscious mind links with
the Eternal Mind, all manner of creativity will begin to flow.
All too often we rely only upon what we know or believe,
when the wisdom of the ages is accessible within us.
Drink from the stillness. Trust that you are being filled.
Wait patiently and your cup will eventually overflow with
all that is needed.

A Vaster Sky

There is a band of consciousness that we
can access that is more subtle than our daily
awareness. It is here that we meet the Gods
and Goddesses of all religions. We can
penetrate this realm through devotion to
any of these Deities who have deeply touched
our imagination. Through them, we find
access to a miraculous world of possibilities.
We are meant to open to realms beyond our
own. As reverence and devotion awakens
in us, we find ourselves expanding into
a vaster sky.

Listen for the Guidance

The world speaks to us in signs and signals.
The guidance may come through the words
of a friend, an event, a hunch, a dream or in
some other way. It is our inner Self that must
interpret the information that comes. Often we
take our cues from the external world without
enough inner reflection. Go inward. Find
the center. Feel for the truth vibrating there.
Listen for the guidance that always comes.

MYSTERIOUS PORTAL

We must learn to take our eyes off the
world outside. We are mesmerized by
what we see. We are ensnared in a web
of daily activities. When we take time for
meditation or prayer, we remember that
we are also connected to a world that is far
more subtle and refined. It is from this world
that true creativity arises. When we quiet
the senses of the body and sink down into
the stillness, the body becomes a mysterious
portal into worlds unknown.

HIDDEN ESSENCE

The stories and myths of the world carry
the deeper wisdom that lies within the psyche
of Creation. These stories are not logical truths;
they are dream landscapes through which we
may travel. Through them the hidden essence
of truth is revealed. Like poems, they are
distillations from those who have entered
into the Mystery and returned to tell the tale.
They cannot speak of what they have seen.
It is too vast for that. They can merely weave
a spell and point a finger in the direction
we must gaze.

Sculptor

Be content to evolve with steady patience. Like a sculptor, you can only chip away one unneeded piece at a time. Recognize an area of life that needs attention and work. Through focused, dedicated attention, what needs to be removed will reveal itself. There is great power once we commit ourselves to healing. Ultimately, all that is unessential will fall away. Our authentic nature emerges. But do not overwhelm yourself. Build slowly and surely, one piece at a time. There will come a day when you will have removed all that is not you.

CONDUITS

Once we create a powerful relationship
between our personality self and our
Higher, energetic Self, our growth accelerates
profoundly. Our intuitive wisdom quickens.
Leaps in understanding begin to occur
with a greater and more refined frequency.
We become conduits for a vaster awareness
than is available to our conscious self.
This is the sacred marriage of body and soul.

ALIGNMENT

A correct alignment of energy in the body
supports the awakening of higher levels
of consciousness. As we stabilize our
consciousness in the belly center, the head
center is no longer cluttered with energies
that are intended to rest in the lower body.
The third eye thereby becomes unstressed.
Our intuitive wisdom becomes activated.
We find ourselves having access to the vast sea
of awareness that exists beyond conscious thought.
When our bodies are thus aligned, our will and
the Will of Heaven will eventually become one.

INTEGRATION

We must unite within our own being
the divine love affair: the sacred marriage
of the God and Goddess, the Father and Mother,
the masculine/feminine principles of Creation.
Only when kindness weds clarity, when mercy
unites with justice and when power yields to
hold and tend the fragile, can we hope to heal
the tragedy of this world. Give all that you have
to this integration of the two aspects that dwell
within you.

DISTILLED BY TIME

When it is time to wait, surrender to the
waiting. There are wisdoms that can only
be born through time. Hidden out of sight,
life is brewing. We cannot force anything
to come. Something that is born before
its time will sicken or die. Embrace time.
Everything you have surrendered will finally
reappear, distilled by time into a deeper
and more powerful offering.

WAVES OF THEIR EMBRACE

Energy is the movement of consciousness.
Consciousness is the eternal Presence at the
 root of energy. When consciousness quickens
energy and energy quickens consciousness,
a whole new separate entity is born. The
yin/yang duality fuses to become a stone,
a bird, a tree. All are creations of the Divine
Feminine and Masculine, of Shakti and Shiva,
of energy and consciousness uniting as one.
From the waves of their loving embrace
a particle is born, a child among their
myriad children.

OUR PRAYERS HAVE POWER

Prayer vibrates the etheric web. If we pray
for another, a vibration flows from our
intention toward the person for whom
we pray. Never underestimate the energy
that is stirred and released through prayer.
The more comfortable we are with prayer,
and the more faith we have that our prayers
have power, the greater will be the intensity
of the vibration we send forth. Take time
to pray. Discover the potency, the wonder
that unfolds.

RITUAL

Ritual is a way to contact the deeper Self.
We become focused and still. We create an
intention and the intensity of that intention
unleashes a force that stimulates the unseen
energy of Life to become active. The more
often a ritual is entered into, the stronger
grows the connection between the seen and
the unseen worlds. The gap between the
intent and the intended, the creator and
the created slowly begins to disappear.

POWER

All Power is a form of magic, and we wield magic
through knowledge of the laws of manifestation.
Power always creates for either good or evil.
What distinguishes Black Magic from White
Magic is motivation. When we desire dominion
over anyone or anything, we are falling into
darkness. When we seek to uplift and enrich
creation, we are using Power to enlighten and
illuminate. Power itself is neutral and amoral.
It is the alchemy of our consciousness that decides
whether Power will create for good or for ill.

ATTRIBUTES

The Absolute, the Source from which all life arises, is far beyond
the duality of this world. It is far beyond the belief in right and wrong.
The Gods and Goddesses that we look to for guidance are a prism
through which we can intuit the attributes of the Great Mystery. Their
qualities of creation, preservation and destruction are only relevant in
this dimension, in this finite world of form. Nonetheless, they help us
approach the Great Emptiness, the timeless, creative Essence that cannot
be named.

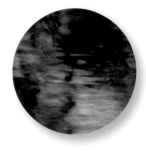

KNOWN AND UNKNOWN

Within us there are two natures. One is an animal nature, which carries
the abilities and limitations of our genetic ancestry. It is an organic being
with access to all that has lived before in the known universe. The other
is an inorganic being, which is connected with the eternal, vast essence
of the Unknown. It is our journey to unite these two beings: our small
self and our Higher Self. The unknown Higher Self enters the known,
offering access to a vaster view. And the known self is refined, enabling
it to be able to travel in realms Unknown.

THE SACRED MARRIAGE

The feminine principle in nature always upholds relationship, while the masculine principle upholds autonomy. The one seeks to merge while the other seeks to individuate. We can only experience true relationship when we are capable of standing alone. And we can only truly stand alone when we realize that we are forever interconnected with everything. We are a paradox of opposing urges. We are both separate from, and one with, all of creation. We must stand alone and we must stand together. This is the sacred marriage.

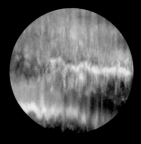

THE VEIL

Our own evolution, our maturation, is a gradual process of remembering, of returning to our rightful alignment with Creation. When the strands of consciousness that make up all of Creation form into an object or a being, the waves of awareness transform into particles of matter, thought and emotion. The very act of being born into the world of form, of being created, causes a veil of forgetfulness to fall over the conscious awareness of that which has been created into something finite. The work of a lifetime is to see the veil, to recognize the veil for what it is, and finally to lift the veil and step through, so that we remember our original state.

MASTER BOTH WORLDS

The world of dreams and the world we
call 'reality' are in truth not that far apart.
They are simply two separate dimensions
built upon energy that has been touched
by two differing levels of awareness. The
conscious mind creates a more stable reality.
The dream world, accessed by the subconscious
mind, is more volatile and unstable. As we
learn to observe and interpret our experiences
in these two realms, we gain an ability to
travel through and master both worlds.
The shaman and the mystic understand
and use this truth.

THE GREAT ATTRACTOR

Love is not a sentimental emotion. Love
is a state of being, a force of the Universe.
Love is the binding energy at the core of all
Creation. Love pulls and holds all things
together. Atoms are drawn to one another
to create themselves into molecules. Molecules
unite into cells, cells into matter, muscle, blood
and bone. Love holds the moon to the earth,
the earth to the sun, the sun to the galaxy.
We exist because of Love. Love is the Great
Attractor, the permanent, binding energetic
fusion that holds all Creation together,
uniting us into One.

KNOWN, UNKNOWN AND UNKNOWABLE

There is that which we know. There is that which is unknown,
but which we can intuit and thus bring into the realm of the known.
And there is the vast realm of that which is completely unknowable.
We can become slaves to the known and never explore the unknown.
We can pursue the unknown relentlessly and never master what is
known. We can enmesh the mind in trying to understand the
unknowable and never accept that it will forever remain beyond the
mind's reach. It is therefore wise to differentiate between the three:
the known, the unknown and the unknowable.

GODS AND GODDESSES

The Gods and Goddesses that exist in all religions everywhere are archetypal energetic portals through which we can approach the unknowable Absolute Mystery. They are expressions of the Love, Light, Life and Law of all things. Each one holds an aspect of what can never be named. The force field that they embody has power to influence Creation. We cannot grasp how this influence occurs, but we do know that it does. We see it, feel it, and experience it. Our faith and trust in the Gods and Goddesses quickens the vibrating matrix to attract, in response to our prayer, that which we need and intend.

THREE CENTERS

The body has three centers: the mind,
the heart and the belly. The center of
gravity for the emotional, mental, physical
and spiritual stability of the body and
personality resides in the belly, the Hara,
the Dantien. The center of gravity for
the psychological, spiritual Self, our
transcendental capacity to intuit and
contemplate abstract reality, dwells in
the center of the head, the third eye.
The center that unites these two centers
of the body and soul is the heart center,
the place of compassionate discernment.

BODY AND SOUL

We are meant to realize and experience
the body and the soul as being one. In this
endeavor we must use every possible aid: breath,
contemplation, meditation, and an ongoing
conscious connection with the inner stillness
that resides within our three centers: the belly,
the heart and the third eye. The body is an
outward expression of the soul. The soul
is an inner resident of the body. Through
strengthening the conscious connection
between body and soul we come to experience
them as being one.

A Key

We cannot understand Creation.
It is much too mysterious. But the more
we love Creation and the more we feel
gratitude, awe and wonder, the more
the Mystery will reveal Herself to us.
She will take us into her confidence.
She will offer a key. We begin to intuit
Her marvels, not through the understanding
of our mind alone, but through the knowing
of our body and the inspiration of our heart.

Great Souls

Great souls have passed through this
plane of existence. We may love and
revere them as the way-showers, for our own
potential can be seen shining in the love and
wisdom that they came to embody. So many
men and women have accomplished what
we, too, will accomplish. They realized that
within and beyond form, all things are one.
This is Self-Realization, the recognition
that our own Self and the Source are one.
Once this is fully experienced, all separation
and strife ceases.

SELF-CONTAINMENT

Power grows through containment.
The more we are able to contain our life
force, rather than suppress it or bleed it away,
the more energy will be generated within.
As we mature, physically, mentally and
emotionally, we become more self-contained.
The more self-contained we are, the more
power we have to call upon. With time, more
spiritual discernment becomes available to
assist us in guiding that power with wisdom.

WIELD IT WELL

Power is amoral. It is dangerous in the
hands of the immature. Those with positive
as well as those with negative intentions can
use power with equal force. Be aware then.
What you intend for others, you unwittingly
intend for yourself. Contain your power.
Allow it to energize and mature you. A day
will come when you will be required to wield
it well.

AGENTS OF CHANGE

To the degree that we are identified
and fixated on our view of this world,
to that degree we are trapped within it.
As we begin to open to greater possibilities,
we invite our perception to become flexible.
This flexibility invites an expanded view
to appear before us. Throughout history
there have been quantum shifts in humanity's
capacity to perceive. We stand at the brink
of such a shift. Some of us are being called
to allow that shift to occur within us.
If you feel called to be one of these agents
of change, make time in your life to
cultivate receptivity.

A WORLD OF WONDER

Like a rolling wheel, our days move on.
The time that passes is gone forever.
We too often grow complacent, living as
if what we see is a commonplace occurrence.
It is not commonplace. Life is a fantastic
phenomenon of awe-inspiring diversity.
Pay attention to the minutiae – the fingernails
of a baby, the sound of the rain at twilight.
Marvel at these small things and gratitude
will come and unfold a pathway into
a world of wonder.

Your Season

When winter is upon the land, there is nothing for the seed to do but wait.

When spring appears, there is nothing for the bud to do but blossom.

When summer unfolds, there is nothing for the fruit to do but ripen.

And when autumn comes, there is nothing for the fruit to do but fall.

This is the way of it. Why cling to or struggle against the season in which

you find yourself? Cultivate equanimity, patience and acceptance,

and you will find joy whatever your season.

THE MIRACLE OF YOUR BEING

The only gift we can give to life is to arrive
in the present moment with the strength
to be open. Every one of us has the opportunity
to bless Creation by fully recognizing that we
are each, precious, unique and extraordinary.
Be truly authentic. Fall in love with the particular
manifestation that is you.
Celebrate, without hubris, the miracle
of your own Being.

GREET THE DAY

Sunrise is a wonderful time to arise, for the sun,
the dew and the birds are awakening with us.
This is a time to open ourselves to the pulse
of creation. Greet the day with thanksgiving
for another opportunity. It is never too late to
have the life you were born to enjoy. No matter
the circumstance. No matter the obstacles that
confront you. Give thanks for the chance to
begin anew.

EVOLUTION

Once you dedicate your human life
to the evolution of your true eternal Self,
all manner of forces come to your aid.
Why judge experience as good or bad
when all experience is composting
for the growth of your Spirit?
Rather than judging events as wanted
or unwanted, become life's ever-watchful
student. Observe, question and be ever-
curious about each moment. Accept the
present as a gift and a lesson for your
ongoing evolution.

MAGNIFICENT TURNING

Give up all complaining. The circumstances
of life constantly flip from desirable to
undesirable and back again. We can learn
to observe the flux and change of each event
with the fascination we might feel for a novel
unfolding. Become the reader. Celebrate
the magnificent turning of events. Acceptance,
like happiness, is a choice and a practice.
Though you may grieve at times, know that
each turn is leading you closer to home.

Allow for New Growth

A rose must be pruned to bloom in
all its fullness. Clinging to what belongs
to the past will stifle our beauty.
Cut away what is done and gone.
Allow new growth to arise from
the emptiness that remains.
There is great power in letting go.
Let go. Have no fear. Fresh wisdom
is born of the courage to surrender.
Certainly something fresh and
beautiful will come to bloom.

Imprints

We are primarily creative beings. Everywhere
we go we leave our mark upon the land,
for good or for ill. No other animal desires
to change what is. This is our great blessing
and our great curse. It separates and alienates
us from all of creation. It crowns and exalts us.
Make no mistake: your life is your offering.
Your daily activities are the imprints you leave
as your gift to life. Make absolutely sure you
are creating, from your deepest desire,
your highest offering.

BE TRANSFORMED

Far better to stand with arms outstretched toward the rising sun, speechless with awe and reverence, than to cling to a religious dogma that must eventually be transformed. To believe that the One God is omnipresent, omnipotent, all-pervading and all-knowing is quite a different reality than to be transfigured by the experience of such a Presence. It is time to let go of all limiting beliefs. It is time to allow ourselves to expand and dissolve into the nameless wonder of it all.

THE LISTENING HEART

Inspiration is with us always. We have only to breathe in, to inspire,
to go inward on the breath for the indwelling Spirit to ignite and come
alive. When we are centered within Self, a quickening occurs. The inner
and outer worlds begin to resonate as one. The creative force that is the
source of all inspiration informs and inspires us. Inspiration can only
be received by an inwardly receptive, listening heart.

IN LOVE WITH THE MYSTERY

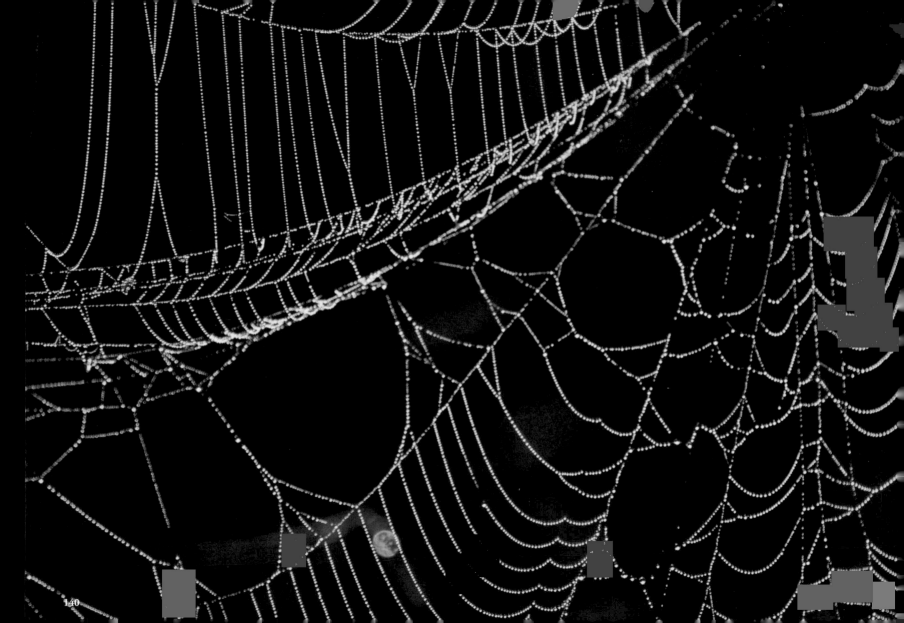

In Love with the Mystery

It is never too late to begin anew. We must allow our self to be forever recreated. In fact, this is the only way to live the spiritual life. Every day, every moment is a doorway into a new possibility. A deeper communion with the Divine unfolds when we choose to open that door. It is one thing to know this to be true, it is quite another to experience that ever-deepening communion. Fall in love with the Mystery. Let it speak from every created thing in every created moment.

LET THE POWER COME

Let the power come. Let ecstasy
erupt. Allow your heart to expand
and overflow with adoration for this
magnificent creation and for the love,
wisdom and power that birthed it all.
Rapture is needed now – rapture,
reverence and grace.

JOY IS THE OCEAN

Joy is a state of being, deeper and
more permeating than happiness
or sadness could ever be. Happiness
is like the sparkle of sunlight on water.
Joy is the ocean itself. Happiness can
be clouded by sorrow. Joy remains
constant through rain or shine.
Emotions come and go like the tides.
Joy is forever present.

THE GREAT SILENCE

Our life in this world is a wheel that
is forever revolving. Nothing in creation
is static. Yet at the center of all this activity,
in the hub of all that is, lies Silence.
Silence, the still, vast, eternal Void,
is filled with unmanifest creative
potential. Let this stillness be the source
of all your action, all your wisdom,
power and compassion. Drop quietly
into this Silence. Here lies the seed
of your becoming. Our destiny quickens
and unfolds in service to, and as an
expression of, the Great Silence.

IDENTIFY WITH THIS

We identify our self with that which will
eventually fade. Our gifts, possessions,
personality, and beliefs are all momentary
appearances on the eternal field of Creation.
That which endures is the formless substance
from which all things emerge. Identify with
this and all separation and loneliness will cease.

LIFE-GIVING SUSTENANCE

Like rain to a thirsty desert,
so is Silence to an overactive mind.
The quiet waters wash away the dust
from the air. They quench our thirst.
Silence stills the emotions. It filters
the essence of soul into every cell
of the body. Allow Silence to be
a constant source of refreshment.
Come to Silence like a hummingbird
comes to the flower's nectar.
Know that there you will find
life-giving sustenance.

STABILITY

If our mind and emotions remain
untamed, we remain incapable of
recognizing or of being aligned with
the Will of Heaven. When we can
maintain a stable neutrality as thoughts
and feelings arise and fall, we will have
established the inner balance that
leads to right action. Cultivate stability.
Once the mind and emotions no longer
war with life, following the Will of Heaven
becomes as natural as breathing.

OCEAN OF AWARENESS

Open the channels through which the Higher Self can flow. Day after day, listen to the deeper feelings and intuitions as they arise. Begin to follow these subtle urgings and, before long, your inner guidance will become clear and fluid. The conscious mind perceives what floats on the surface of the waters of Awareness. The Higher Mind has access to a vast body of knowing that swims beneath that surface. In time the surface and the depth will come together and be experienced as the one great ocean of Awareness.

BECOME EMPTY

Love of the Unnameable will in the end lead to the cross and to the
bodhi tree. We must be crucified to be born anew. We must be brought
down to be exalted. We must be shattered to be made whole again.
It is the way of it. All of our false gods: wealth, fame, prestige, must
be washed of significance before we are able to reach the other shore.
Let your undoing happen without resistance. There is no greater glory
than to become empty.

FREEDOM

The greatest spiritual achievement is to
maintain a sustained inner equilibrium
in the midst of the fluctuating upheavals
and demands of daily life. Our moment-
by-moment behavior and mood is the
measurement of our true freedom.
Cultivate a calm and peaceful disposition.
Practice acceptance and surrender to life
as it is and spiritual freedom will be yours.

THE UNKNOWABLE

We flatter ourselves by believing we have
discovered something new when, in truth,
we have merely uncovered what was always there.
Everything we need lies hidden in the unknown.
The unknowable will forever remain a mystery.
We penetrate the unknown by cultivating inner
silence and focused intent. Slowly, after years
of active waiting and vigilant observation,
the door will appear. The unknown forever
lures us to that door, but it is the Unknowable
that humbles us and eventually pulls us through.

GO BEYOND

Time spent in quiet contemplation
is a precursor to inner silence. And inner
silence, the ability to still the mind of its
incessant ruminating, is the precursor to
awakening. How can we know who or
what we really are unless we can go beyond
our limiting beliefs and perceptions?
Beyond duality, beyond right or wrong,
good or bad, dark or light, lies a world of unity.
Here all is seen as one great vibrating energetic
field of which all of creation is composed.
And beyond this vibrating field: a void
of silent, empty, unknowable stillness.

THE SUBTLER SENSES

The reality of this world is revealed through
the five senses of the body in which we travel.
Do not limit yourself to what can be seen,
heard, touched, tasted or smelled. Other
realities can be revealed through senses
that we have either lost or not yet found.
Cultivate the subtler senses. Listen for the
sound beyond hearing, the sight beyond
what your eyes can perceive. Sense the
Presence beyond understanding and new
worlds will be revealed.

RESERVOIR OF KNOWLEDGE

Below the surface of the conscious
mind there lies a reservoir of knowledge.
Few take the time to drink from these waters.
Those who do, become channels through
which inspiration flows into the world.
If you dip daily in this well, all manner
of awareness will come to you. This is the
realm from which creativity flows. Dive deep.
Drink deep. And the deep thirst that haunts
us all will be quenched.

NOTHING IS EXCLUDED

In our lifetime we are meant to expand in
consciousness. We are a pebble dropped
in a pool creating ripples that expand.
Each ripple goes beyond, yet includes
the ripple that came before. Nothing
is left behind. Nothing is ever excluded.
Each experience expands into greater
wisdom. Consciousness moves toward
ever-greater inclusion. Ultimately, there
are no mistakes. Everything serves the
expansion of awareness.

Unseen Forces

When we know that there are unseen
forces waiting to support our unfolding,
we move with greater ease along the
pathway of awakening. We are supported
not because we are favored, but because
we believe. We watch for signs and signals.
We listen to our intuitions and dreams.
We know there is wisdom and guidance
waiting to be found. We listen with receptivity,
not only to the world that speaks to our
five senses, but also to the world that
communicates from beyond the veil.

Spiraling Dancers

Loss makes way for gain. Gain fills the
place that once was filled by what is lost.
Neither is more important than the other.
They move like spiraling dancers as we evolve.
Like two pistons of an engine, they empower
our lives with change. When we accept
one or the other with equal equanimity,
we have finally surrendered and become
one with Life.

PERFECT MOMENT

Tempests come and go. Hurricanes lay waste the land. Earthquakes shatter our dreams. And always spring returns. New buds form and birdsong fills the air. In spite of all that we impose upon ourselves, or all that is imposed upon us, the world is simply magnificent. Whether a gale is raging or a warm breeze is ruffling your hair, embrace, endure, and appreciate this perfect moment now.

GREET EACH ONE

Every sentient being, every rock, plant, or animal is unique in all of creation. When we greet each being with a sense of the miraculous, our life becomes a song of praise. Everything finds blessing in our presence. Does there need to be a greater joy or purpose than this?

Inner Guidance

In every generation there have been
great souls, recognized and unrecognized.
They are completing their own awakening
through service to all. Some of them step
forward onto the stage of history. Others
evolve quietly in the stillness of a reclusive
life. But each of these great ones has known
this truth: their destiny's fulfillment and
their service to the whole depends solely
upon their invincible willingness to stay
true to their inner guidance, wherever
it might lead.

The Rolling Wheel

Remember that death is the precursor
to renewal. What is dying now was once
the renewal for something else that had
to fade. Like a wheel rolling, every experience,
every created thing and every life is born,
lifted up, and moved forward, only to descend,
dissolve, and begin again. Nothing you are
experiencing now is important in and of itself.
It is important only because it keeps the great
wheel of life turning. Beware of identifying
with your story. You will only become stuck
in the mire of attachment to the self you
are now living. Merely see it for what it
is and then roll on.

Inner Stillness

Inner stillness is the prerequisite to
remembering. We cannot penetrate the
veil of forgetfulness until we still our
internal energies. The assumption that
what we know as true is true, keeps us
from being fluid, just as consciousness
is fluid. As we become a constant listening,
the intricate wonder of who we actually
are, in all its vibratory simplicity, is revealed.

Silent Emptiness

The great gift that meditation offers
is a pathway along which we can travel
to reach the great Emptiness. In this
great Emptiness, stress dissolves, thoughts
become still, and emotions subside. Here
in the vast stillness, as in an empty womb,
lies the creative potential for new life and
energy to arise. Take time daily to become
a silent emptiness and, in that emptiness,
a creative potency will begin to brew.

ACTIONS FLOW IN HARMONY

Nature is always showing us lessons
of balance. The tide goes out and then
returns, out of death something is reborn.
So many patterns, so many cycles
of renewal. When our lives come into
balance, we feel content to accept the
changing fortunes of life, as the earth
must accept the ever-changing weather
patterns that come and go. There is little
need for talking. Our actions flow in
harmony with the moment. And our
presence becomes the teaching.

MOVEMENT OF LIFE

The sound of running water
or the sound of a whistling wind
soothe because they energetically
connect us to the never-ending
movement of life. There is a current,
a wave of creation that sustains all
things. This is the flow from which
all manifestation arises, only to depart
once more. It is the changing creative
flux of the universe in the changeless
womb of the Eternal Essence.

Infinite and Finite

When we contemplate the nature of a mountain, we can glimpse the outer expression of our own inner core: still, patient, strong and ancient. We must sink our feet into the earth, feel the solidity of the rock on which we stand. Our mind may be able to dance upon the winds of Heaven, but our body must be grounded deep within the material foundation from which it is made. In this way we hold the paradox of being both infinite and finite at the same time, and we can fully experience the grand drama through which we are passing.

ETERNITY

In the timeless reality called Eternity,
where no time and all time exists as one,
all that has ever been, all that is now
and all that is yet to come is everywhere
simultaneously present. Time only exists
in the finite world. Eternity cannot be
created or destroyed. It simply is. All things
and events exist in this present moment. All of
our ancestors and descendants are with us now.
Allow the immensity of timelessness to
permeate your consciousness and you will
be transformed by the marvel that nothing
and no one can ever be lost or found.
Everything and everyone is here, now.

THE FINAL SURRENDER

To be a portal through which love flows
into the world is the final surrender.
We can be equally compassionate with
all people, those who would seek to harm
as well as those who would only bless.
This is the ultimate freedom and attainment.
For then we see the Creator in all of Creation,
face-to-face, and every face worthy of the
greatest honor.

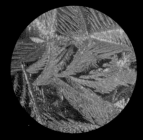

JOY

Beneath sorrow and happiness there lies
the realm of joy. Joy is deeper than any
emotion. It is a state of Being. When we
receive life exactly as it is, whether we
are happy or sad about the circumstance,
we find that beneath these fleeting
emotions there is a wellspring of joy.
This joy knows and celebrates the mystery
in which we are privileged to participate.

AWAKEN INTO WONDER

The ancient mysteries are all but lost to us.
Ecstasy and wonder, awe and reverence
barely touch the life of the ordinary person.
We have lost our ability to fall speechless
before the glory of creation. Paradise is lost.
We regain Paradise when we shed our cynicism,
when we become innocent once more by
falling in love with Mystery. This is our
essential task: to awaken into wonder.

INNER GUIDANCE

Life can become a fluid relationship between
the relative world of form and that which exists
beyond the veil. We can have glimpses of true
knowing and insight through opening our
emotional, mental, physical and spiritual bodies
to other levels of reality. The mystery of creation
becomes the Teacher. And our small, ego-self
becomes the Student. We can stand in awe of
the vast, yet available, wisdom of existence and
follow its inner guidance.

WED TO THE WILL OF HEAVEN

Once the body is stabilized, the soul becomes
more active. We enter the stillness of the heart.
A universe of quiet compassion and truth
unfolds. Our personal will becomes wed to
the Will of Heaven. All our actions in the
world, whether grand or seemingly insignificant,
generate from this Source. We are intended
to be a conduit through which the essence
of Love and Truth flows from the Beyond
and pours its blessing into Creation.

THE SAME LIGHT

Everything around us has come out
of no-thing and will dissolve back into
no-thing. Even stars are born and die.
Everything is made of the same Light,
the same sound waves moving.
Everything takes form for a brief
time in space and then dematerializes
once more. Cultivate awareness of the
formless essence from whence you have
come and to which you will return.
And the Mystery of Life will begin to
unfold before you in all its magnificence.

SELF-REALIZATION

When we realize that the body and soul
are actually one entity vibrating at different
frequencies then we experience Self-Realization.
On earth, we have a duality that only exists
here. For but a moment, our formless Self
has taken on form to experience this
fascinating dimension of manifestation.
The small self is the Eternal Self having
an adventure in time and space.

MAGNIFICENCE

The mind is fashioned to discover
the glorious creativity behind Creation.
The heart is fashioned to expand and fall
rapturous before the wonder of Creation.
The belly is fashioned to include and
encompass the passions of Creation.
This is our journey here on earth.
For when our centers are open, the
magnificence of the world appears.
All longing for more ceases to ensnare.
It is a delicious freedom.

THE BLESSING

The end of desire awakens the blessing.
We see life as perfect with all its joys
and challenges. We become capable of
penetrating its secrets. We find that what
was hidden becomes revealed. What was
unfathomable becomes simple and direct.
This is the blessing that can only be
known through unconditional gratitude.

THE VAST SEA

Everything in life is an energetic wave upon
a vast sea of consciousness. All physical reality
is made of wave particles appearing and
disappearing upon the surface of this endless
sea. They blink in and out. They rise and fall.
Our lives, too, are a fluid impulse in limitless
space. We appear for a moment and then we
dissolve and return back into the sea. Identify
yourself as being the vast sea of consciousness,
and the wave you are riding at this moment
will lose its power to overthrow you.

THE CENTER OF THE PARADOX

It is the work of a lifetime to stand in the
center of the paradox and be undisturbed.
We must hold, at one and the same time,
that this life is full of meaning, while it has
no meaning at all. We are hopeless to change
anything and yet we are Life's only hope.
Everything we build will be torn down.
Everything that is lost will return again.
When both sides of the paradox are held
with equal reverence, we are truly free.

THE ETERNAL ESSENCE OF BEING

We are a becoming. There is no shore to which
we must journey. There is no place to which we
must arrive. We are an ever-evolving phenomenon,
changing, spiraling, transforming. Consciousness
is not a place to which we are going. It is the very
substance, the essence of all we are. Our body,
mind, emotion and soul are fluctuations of
awareness within an endless vibration. We are
sparks of intelligence at play. To be resurrected
in every moment of every day is to grasp the
perpetual nature of becoming and the eternal
essence of being.

MIRACLE

The mystery of our appearance here
on a planet revolving through space
is a mystery that will always remain.
We cannot comprehend or understand it.
We can only experience it at deeper and
deeper levels. As we cultivate wonder,
awe and reverence, the heart opens to
receive the miracle of it all. We finally
awaken to realize that we are, in fact,
simply an intricate part of the Great Mystery.

AMAZEMENT

Our body is a cell in the body of the earth.
The earth is a cell in the body of the galaxy.
The galaxy is a cell in the body of the universe.
And the universe is a cell in the body of
the Infinite. The Divine Play is too vast
to even begin to comprehend. But it is not
too vast to celebrate. Allow awe and wonder
to rise. Gaze on this magnificent creation
with amazement and thanksgiving.
You have but this one moment in
Eternity to experience the extraordinary
manifestation before you right now.
This moment will pass, never to come again.
Don't let it pass without appreciating it fully.

FILAMENTS OF AWARENESS

As the veil of forgetfulness grows thinner,
we see that everything in nature is alive and
conscious. The stones and trees, the waters
and the fire, the winds, the animals, all are
composed of the same filaments of awareness.
We can communicate with all of life because
we, too, are made of the same strands of
consciousness. We have only to still the mind,
to watch and listen, and the energetic lines
of connection that bind all of life together,
will appear. We will experience the One
Awareness that resonates in and through
all of Creation.

LIFE AS IT IS

Before enlightenment, chop wood, carry water. After enlightenment, chop wood, carry water. Enlightenment does not necessarily change our outer reality, but it completely transforms our inner experience of that reality. We become illuminated with the simplicity of life as it is. We go about the same daily activities but with no resistance to the joys, sorrows or demands of those activities. Our preference for life being this way or that dissolves, and we become fluid and awake, able to experience, even celebrate, each and every moment. In other words, we surrender and find peace.

The Wellspring

If we take time daily to enter the silence,
a passageway to the eternal is forged.
We engage a sense of familiarity,
even friendship and camaraderie
with that which cannot be named.
An essence, a source of power and
creativity, begins to permeate our
being, bringing a sense of purpose
and relaxation into all we do.
Silence is the wellspring of all there is.
From silence comes sound.
From darkness comes light.
From stillness comes movement.
From nothing, everything.

Mystery

At the root of every spiritual tradition,
we find the mystics: those men and women
in love with the Mystery. They enter the
essential wisdom known to and revealed
by the founder of whichever path they tread.
Here at the root of the tree, after a long journey,
they come face to face with the Unknowable.
And looking into the vast wonder of that
which cannot be named, they bow in awe
and surrender, humbled and elevated by a
Mystery too awe-inspiring to even conceive.

INNER WATERS OF WISDOM

The greatest teacher is our own
soul's connection with the Source.
To access wisdom, distortions within
our human nature must be removed:
beliefs that do not serve, emotional
attachments that cloud. We arrive in
the present moment with no agenda
of our own making. Here in the eternal
present, a fountain begins to rise from
within. It is the inner waters of wisdom,
the essential wellspring of remembering.

LUMINOUS BEAUTY

As we begin to orient ourselves toward
our eternal nature, our day-to-day
reality takes on a dreamlike quality.
We see each moment as a pearl strung
upon a string of pearls, each one perfect,
each one disappearing as quickly as it arose.
There is no longer a need to hang
onto its luminous beauty. For we know
that in the next moment, a new pearl
of equal price will appear from the sea
of endless possibility.

MEDITATION

When a storm is raging and the waves are tumultuous, it is wise to dive deep down to where the water is calm. If we remain on the surface, we will be tossed and turned. But if, like the whale, we retreat to the quiet depths of our own Being, our true home, we will find rest and peace there. Once refreshed, we can resurface. This is the value of meditation. We can weather any storm with greater ease if we allow ourselves to retreat when necessary to the still, vast depths within.

No Separation

The stories of Buddha and Jesus are stories
of our own potential. "Greater things than
I have done, ye shall do," Jesus promised.
We are meant to recognize that we are born
of the Divine, created in God's image, one with
the Source. We may be small and insignificant
on one level, but we are vast beyond measure
on another. One day, after lifetimes of struggle,
we will let go of our resistance and accept our
sovereignty. When no separation exists between
our small self and our Infinite Self, we will take
our place beside the Buddha and Jesus and
know we were never separate from them
in the first place.

Our Purpose

The purpose of life is to allow the Divine Self
to have full expression through and within
our human self. We are meant to incarnate
the Infinite into the finite. The saints and
mystics knew this to be true and they aligned
their natures with the Divine Nature. In so
doing, they created the possibility upon which
we now stand. We are intended, through our
own development, to move evolution forward
into ever-greater possibilities. We are the
conduits through which life transforms
and evolves. Life expands as we expand.

PAUL HORN

World-renowned flutist, Paul Horn, is a versatile and widely popular recording artist with over fifty albums to his credit. His famous recording, *Inside the Taj Mahal,* ushered in a whole new genre of music and positioned Paul as the founding father of New Age music. His career, spanning six decades, has been an inspiring odyssey of world travel, expansive musical creativity, psychological evolution, and spiritual transformation.

Ann Mortifee and Paul Horn were married in 2006 and share their life on a Gulf Island in B.C. and in Arizona.
www.paulhornmusic.com

COURTNEY MILNE

Courtney Milne is a master photographer, artist, author, educator, keynote speaker, and philanthropist. He has published 12 books of photography, including *The Sacred Earth.* Milne's multi-media shows have attracted audiences worldwide, and his photographs have been shown in more than 200 exhibitions. In keeping with Courtney's mission to "inspire wonder and impassioned living," each of his deeply sensitive images provides a stunning complement to the passages of *In Love with the Mystery.*

Courtney and his wife Sherrill Miller live in Saskatchewan.   www.courtneymilne.com

In Love With The Mystery Companion CD

The music on this recording was totally unrehearsed and spontaneous. Although the words were previously written, they were not shared with the musicians before we began. We merely became quiet and then moved into a free improvisation. The Muse visited the four of us in Paul Baker's studio that day and we all feel so very grateful and blessed.

MUSICIANS:

Flutes: Paul Horn

Guitar: Ed Henderson

Keyboards: Miles Black

Vocals: Ann Mortifee

Produced by: Ann Mortifee and Ed Henderson

Engineered by: Paul Baker

Additional Engineering: Dave Meszaros

Recorded at: Baker Street Studios

Mastered by: Graemme Brown, Zen Mastering

TRACKS:

1. Enter the Silence

2. Mysterious Journey

3. Sacrificing Resistance

4. The Listening Heart

5. In Love With the Mystery

6. Celebrate

Total: 46 minutes

5.1 Surround Sound and Stereo